# DETROIT STEEL

# DETROIT STEEL

## THE NEW AGE OF THE GREAT AMERICAN PERFORMANCE CAR

David Fetherston

**Dedication**
For Ben - muscle cars for the muscle man.

First published in Great Britain in 1994
by Osprey, an imprint of Reed Consumer
Books Limited, Michelin House,
81 Fulham Road, London SW3 6RB
and Auckland, Melbourne,
Singapore and Toronto.

© Reed International Books Ltd 1994

ISBN 1 85532 323 0

Editor Shaun Barrington
Page Design Paul Kime/Ward Peacock
Partnership
Produced by Mandarin Offset
Printed and bound in Hong Kong

# Acknowledgements

As a car-crazy ten year old, I knew every American car at the blink of an eye. The shine and dazzle was backed up with comfort and cubic inches. I wanted one, any one. Today I have driven just about all of them, and I remain a dedicated lover of the cubic inches and luxury that only Detroit builds into its cars.

I would like to thank all the public relations folks with Cadillac, Pontiac, Chevrolet, Buick, Oldsmobile, GM, Ford, Chrysler, in both Detroit and Los Angeles for their time and interest in helping us get this book done. I would also like to thank Page One Automotive for their dedicated and reliable help, Mike Chase for his able assistance with the photography, Nanette Simmons for her assistance and persistence, Tom Lankard for his editorial review of the text, Cori Ewing for his help with captions and photography. A special thanks goes to Gloria for all her steadfastness and editorial help in coaxing this project to completion.

Virtually all the photography I shot for the book was done on a Mamiya RB 6X7 Pros S camera system. It's a great machine — just like a Cadillac. Once again all the film was Fuji RDP 100, superbly processed by The Lab in Santa Rosa, California. The remainder of the photos came from manufacturers' sources.

**Front cover**
Reeves Callaway's ZR-1-based 750 hp Super Speedster, built for Dr Larry Joel as the ultimate Callaway Corvette. 0-60 sub four seconds

**Back cover**
Driver's dream, at a guess, a Chrysler strategic planner's nightmare: the magnificent Viper. (See page 67)

**Half title page**
Power for the AREX (see page 121) comes from a 5.7 litre Chevrolet V8 with twin Banks turbos, twin intercoolers, trick heads and electronic fuel injection

**Title page**
1994 Pontiac Trans Am. (See page 38)

For a catalogue of all books published by Osprey Automotive
please write to:

**The Marketing Department, Reed Consumer Books,
1st Floor, Michelin House, 81 Fulham Road, London SW3 6RB**

# Introduction

The title 'Detroit Iron' has often been bandied about in some derogatory ways over the years. But time has proven the soothsayers quite wrong. America can and does build some of the finest cars in the world. The Europeans have long laid claim to the best, the fastest and the most luxurious automobiles; meantime the Americans have been quietly refreshing their quality, performance and design so that today, they can confidently step up to the challenge. Take the Viper, the Corvette, the Mark VIII Lincoln and the Cadillac STS. All these are at the head of their class when it comes to performance, luxury and handling.

While the Europeans and Japanese manufacturers have been working with small capacity, high revving engines for years, Detroit builders have always worked on big cubic inch engines that offer enormous power at relatively low rpm.

The Viper's output figures demonstrate this perfectly: 400 hp at 4600 rpm backed up to 450 ft/lb torque at 3600 rpm. In sheer performance terms, Detroit delivers such great power-to-weight ratios as 8.2:1 for the Viper and 8.5:1 for the Corvette ZR-1, while Ferrari with its super Testarossa lags way behind with 9.6:1.

This need for speed is deeply rooted in American hot rod history. But Detroit is not all horsepower; American manufacturers also have a style all of their own. They can mix performance, luxury, style and handling into a package that sells like the proverbial hot cakes. Cadillac's wildly successful new Seville STS sold out in the first nine months of its production in '92 even after Cadillac built an extra 30,000 units to satisfy the overwhelming demand. Ford have also had great success with their Mustang GT, which has been in production for close to ten years. Nevertheless it is now set for replacement in 1994. Powered by a fuel injected, 225 hp V8, the Mustang GT offered handling and style, five-speed transmission and sports interior for less than US $20,000.

The Corvette from Chevrolet also tells a special tale. More than one million have been built since 1954. In that time, the Corvette has evolved from a show car with a 'suburban' straight six engine to one of the most brutally powerful and adhesive sports coupés ever built.

American performance still has its super-tuners and hot rod elements. Reeves Callaway's twin-turbo and SuperNatural Corvettes are performance mind blowers; the Vector supercar can outrun a Ferrari F40; the Consulier Sport C4 is a street and race champ; and the AREX roadster is simply wild. All of these are shining lights in the performance firmament. America can confidently step up to bat in the second half of the decade with a line-up of players who can mount a daunting challenge to the rest of the automotive world.

**Right**
Just two years from auto show sensation to roadster reality; V10 Viper

# Contents

**General Motors Corporation**   8

**Chrysler**   66

**Ford**   90

**Specialty Builders**   112

# General Motors Corporation

The mighty manufacturing mammoth, General Motors, has long been America's automotive leader. Mostly its vehicles have been for mass transit; getting folks to work and home. But GM's image is far more intense. Its best products come from its luxury and sports car divisions. After all, think sports cars and you think Corvette and Camaro; think luxury and Cadillac Seville STS immediately races to mind. GM is much more than the sum of Cadillac and Corvette, but with those two products leading their sales divisions in an industry now awash with great products, it's hard not to see only the cream which floats at the top. Buick and Oldsmobiles also have some interesting vehicles in the sporty car class, but it's the guys from Pontiac who are putting 'the bang' back into affordable street performance with neat new products like the Grand Am V6 GT coupé.

*The Cadillac Allante sports car originally came with the regular 200 hp production, 4.5 litre all-aluminum Cadillac V8. But for '93 it received the new Northstar multi-cam, multi-valve V8. The body was designed and built by Pininfarina in Italy, being air freighted to Cadillac in Detroit for final assembly at the Hamtramck assembly plant. This Cadillac is the only vehicle that is half-built on two continents. Selling for around US $60,000 a copy, the Allante is not produced en masse and limited production has made it an exclusive product that has found many delighted buyers*

**Above**

The car that has returned Cadillac to market leadership, the Seville STS. This stunning, smooth looking sedan is the work of the Cadillac Advanced Design Studio headed up by Dennis Little. Released in '92 as a completely new model, its fine lines are beautifully proportioned and sophisticated. Gone are the squared-off lines which have been a Cadillac trade mark for the last decade. From the driver's seat it's also a completely new ball game. It offers a chassis platform that handles like a Jaguar and delivers the comfort of a Mercedes; and a cabin with the ergonomics of a BMW. With 200 hp on tap the STS does get up and go, but with the '93 platform offering the new 300 hp V8, Mercedes 500 drivers will no longer be 'king of the road' when it comes to hyper-luxury performance

**Right**

The Cadillac Eldorado Touring Coupe is a two-door knock-off of the fabulous Seville STS sedan. As much as they look like brother and sister, none of the body panels are interchangeable, although they are based on the same platform and drivetrain. Power is supplied by a 200 hp all-aluminum V8 driving the front wheels. Aimed at the luxury buyer who wants sporty handling and comfort all wrapped into one package, the Eldorado Touring Coupe is a superbly comfortable five passenger tourer that combines its (electronically limited) top speed of 125 mph with a handling platform that makes driving from LA to New York a painless process

**Above**

The Chevrolet Corvette ZR-1 has been called 'king of the hill' and 'the baddest 'Vette of all'. Both titles suit this monster. Hidden in what is basically a production Corvette body and chassis is a Lotus-developed/Mercury Corporation-built all-aluminum V8 which develops 375 smog-legal hp. The ZR-1 can whip from 0 to 60 mph in 4.4 seconds, clip the quarter mile in sub-13 second runs and run to 174 mph flat strap. The latest generation of Corvette retains its unique American themes of muscular horsepower, rugged construction and tyre-frying performance. Built in Bowling Green, Kentucky, the Corvette is the master blaster of the two seat production coupés. No other super car has ever been built in such numbers over so many years

**Right**

The ZR-1 V8 is one of GM's great engine achievements. Designed as a 5.7 litre/350 cubic inch motor, it develops close to 400 hp and is capable of wailing to 7000 rpm while ripping out a massive 360 ft/lb of torque. Internally it is a very sophisticated motor with all-aluminum block and heads using cast iron liners. The head features two cams per bank with four valves per cylinder. Equipped with a stock six-speed transmission the ZR-1 engine delivers about as big a kick in the pants as any sports car could ever hope to slap down onto the road

**Left**

The Corvette LT1 debuted in '92 with a new 300 hp motor, revised suspension and interior and a new traction control system. Called ASR, or Acceleration Slip Regulator, it gives the Corvette such a traction edge that the development engineers were pacing four- wheel-drives on snowy highways in the depths of the Michigan winters during development. The current Corvette features revised bodywork with a re-styled nose and rear quarter which matches the ZR-1. On the skid pad the Corvette is unstoppable. It can produce a .90 lateral G and brake from 60 mph in 109 feet. From a driver's point of view it's all thumbs up. The variable rate steering, massive 17-inch tyres, multi-link upper and lower control arm suspension with transverse glassfibre mono-leaf rear springs and electronic shock control combine to produce a level of handling that can only be equated with a tube of Crazy Glue and a F1 racer

**Above**

The interior on the new LT1 is identical to the ZR-1 version. It comes with a six-speed shift or four speed automatic. The dash has a display of electronic and mechanical instruments in analog and digital. An air bag is standard on the driver's side, and the seven-way power seats grip every part of the back and lower torso. Climb in, buckle up and go; the Corvette is undoubtedly the World's Best Sports Car

**Above**

The Corvette's sweet lines are shown neatly with this rear shot. Four big tail lights have become a mark of the Corvette and over the years have developed into a fully styled and integrated section of the soft rear tailpiece which covers the hidden impact bumper. The sloping rear glass opens out 'hatch-back' style for access to the luggage compartment

**Left**

The LT1 300 hp V8 is truly one of the great engines of the nineties. Born out of the original small block V8 of the mid fifties, this latest generation is a sweet, smooth and powerful performer. The Corvette is available in two body styles, a coupé with a removable targa roof section and a roadster version with a full folding fabric top

**Above left**

The Corvette Indy, designed and built in 1986, was a ground-breaking design for Chevrolet. The current Corvette had been on the market for two years, but Chevrolet were trying to get a feel for how the next generation due for release in the mid nineties would look and perform. Powered by the new Indy Chevrolet Ilmor, the Indy design had the V8 sitting sideways ahead of the rear wheels. The Indy was built with the help of Lotus, who fabricated two running prototypes for both testing and display. The suspension is a new Lotus-designed, hi-tech Active system which, with the touch of a button, can change the handling and ride from a Cadillac to a F1 race car. The next generation of Corvette is still several years away, but you can bet your bottom dollar some of the themes you see in the Indy and the CERV III will appear in that vehicle

**Left**

The Corvette III, or California Corvette as it was originally known, is the latest in the series of experimental Corvette prototypes to be made public. It is the first experimental roadster since the new Corvette in 1953. Its release in 1992 gave us a feeling that a new generation of Corvettes due out in the next three to four years may well look something like this stunning beast. Styled by John Mack, Jim Beick and Ben Salvador at the GM West Coast

Advanced Designs Concepts Center in Thousand Oaks, California, the California Corvette features all the latest comfort ideas, handling tricks and aerodynamic aids. The roll bar features a 'pop-up' wing with a high mounted stop light; the chassis is a semi-monocoque tub while the body is glassfibre – a Corvette tradition – and the wheels are a unique 18 inch and 19 inch three spoke design

**Above**

Chevrolet have been working on Corvette dreams for the nineties using the CERV III as a prototype model to develop new ideas. Some of the body was built in Italy with most of the chassis work done by Lotus in England. The new four-cam engines are built in the US. This international engineering input has made these Corvettes into a most impressive series of fine American exotics. The CERV III (Corporate Engineering Research Vehicle III), is not just another show car. It is a fully functional rolling test bed for new sports car ideas. It can deliver a blistering level of performance. Chevrolet claim that the CERV III is capable of 0-60 mph in 3.9 seconds with a top speed of 225 mph. It is powered by a twin turboed, ZR-1 four cam, 32 valve Corvette motor

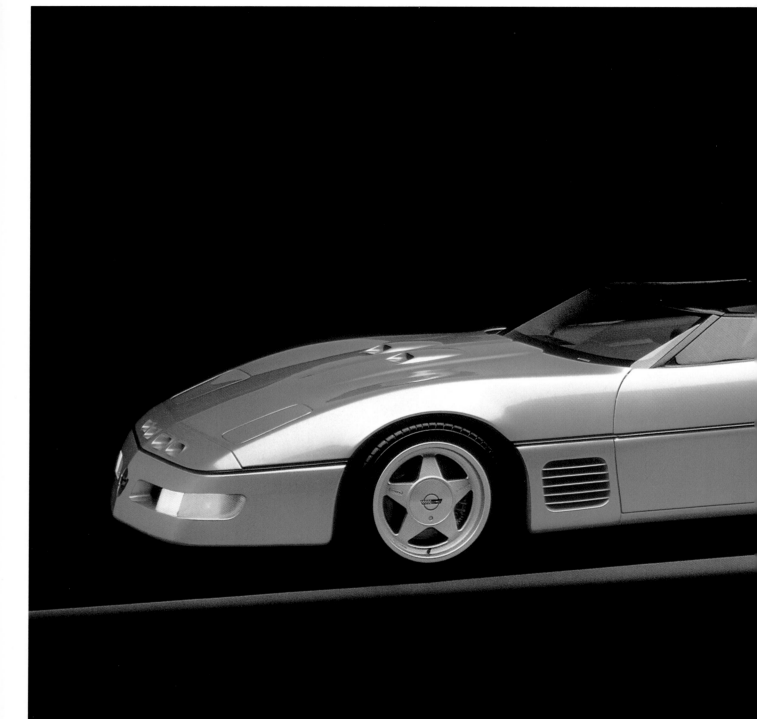

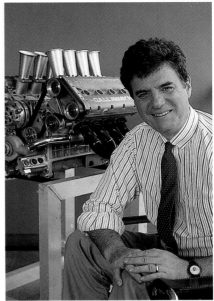

**Above**
Reeves Callaway is the American Ruf or
Cosworth. Callaway started out as a
weekend racer, progressed to National
Formula Vee Champion and went on to
develop a series of turbo kits for
performance cars. But his fame these
days is as the super car tuner with the
talent and ability to build some of the
fastest, most stylish sports cars in the
world

**Left**
After producing 520 twin turbo
Corvettes, Callaway Cars are building
their new Speedster. Based on the same
principles of power and style, the
Speedster is a stunning cousin to the
fabulous Callaway coupé. Callaway takes
a Corvette convertible, slices off the
windshield, installs a swept-back
speedster-style windshield, adds their
own Aero body kit and fixes a pair of
aerodynamic headrests over the old
luggage space area. The result is one of
the most attractive Corvettes ever

**Above**

*Reeves Callaway is one of the great sports car 'tuners'. The Germans may have Ruf and the Brits their Cosworth, but the Yanks have Callaway. Callaway Cars have been building twin-turbo Corvettes for quite a few years until the '93 year models were listed as an RPO or Regular Production Option on the Corvette order form. This stunning Teal Green Roadster was the first 'drop-top' from Callaway but it came with all the bells and whistles including the California street legal 400 hp twin-turbo V8 which can slam the roadster from 0-60 mph in 4.4 seconds*

**Left**

*The twin-turbo Callaway V8 motor produces 400 hp from a pair of Roto Master turbos, inter-coolers and fuel injection. It was developed by Chief Engineer at Callaway, Tim Good, during an extensive research project which blended the traditional power band of the V8 with the turbo's high-energy output at maximum torque. This new performance envelope now delivers its punch with devastating smoothness right across the power range. Top speed in the coupé is 191 mph and in the roadster 176 mph*

**Above**

The Chevrolet Monte Carlo concept car is another slice of the future from Chevy. Its round organic lines feature sub-.30 Cd ratings and DOHC V6 power. The huge 'glasshouse' roof offers a fine view from the spacious and well-refined interior. Designed as a futuristic family sports coupé, the Monte Carlo may well be just more than window dressing. Chevrolet are on a drive to make a whole new generation of automobiles to replace some ageing lines, while upgrading their family big-car image

**Right**

The Chevrolet Cavalier Z24 convertible has been a favourite budget-buy among convertible owners for several years. With a base price of US $14,000, the Cavalier has shown the way to cheaper, more enjoyable driving for many folks. Packaged as the Z24, it comes with an uprated Level III sports suspension, alloy sports wheels and tyres, improved interior comforts and the power of a 3.1 litre 140 hp V6. While this may not seem like an impressive number for a sporty convertible, the Z24 with its handling package and V6 does a fine job of tearing up the road

**Above left**

The Lumina Z34 coupé body was developed for NASCAR racing and, for anyone who watched the movie Days of Thunder, the heroes drove them to win. The Lumina has not made the in-roads into the market that Chevrolet had hoped for. But it has sold well enough to stay in the market place for four model years. Only in its latest generation has the Lumina Coupe finally delivered the goods its looks pretended to promise. Powered by a 210 hp DOHC V6, the Z34 has snap and crackle with a 'Euro' suspension package that can take you through the twisties at a rate of speed high enough to get your blood pressure up and the hormones racing. But its power delivery leaves much to be desired as its performance envelope only opens out at high rpm. The Z34 features a special body kit, wheels and interior trim

**Left**

The Chevrolet Beretta GTZ is certainly a good looking coupé. Propelled by the 180 hp multi-valve Quad Four engine and five-speed manual transmission, the GTZ is the most powerful Beretta of the line-up. For those wanting a smoother, more refined feel, a lower power V6 is optional. This engine develops

140 hp over 185 ft/lb of torque. Acceleration is brisk. The Quad Four and the V6 and the high performance handling suspension that comes with the GTZ does a reasonable job of getting the coupé through the bends. ABS is also a new addition, as is the driver's side air bag. The GTZ can seat four in comfort and five at a squeeze, and while it certainly looks the part of a slick sports coupé, hand on heart, it fails to live up to its looks as a true 'road burner'

**Above**

The 454 SS super truck from Chevrolet has been a smash hit. Based on the C/K1500, the 454 SS is powered by the famous 'Big Block' Chevrolet 454 (7.4 litre) cubic inch V8 engine. It develops a low 255 hp off its throttle body fuel injection, but like all Big Blocks it offers masses of torque with 405 ft/lb readily available. A four-speed automatic is stock as is the limited-slip-differential and sports handling package. Originally only available in black, the 454 SS is now a three-colour model with red and white also available. Chrome-plated steel wheels and an aero-body kit is also part of the 454 SS. Inside, it comes with a pair of layback bucket seats, a super stereo and full instrumentation

**Above**

The new Camaro Z28 Convertible joined the Chevrolet line in '94. Built at the St. Therese Assembly plant in Canada, this is the fourth generation of Camaro since its '67 introduction. The convertible features eight special steel sub-structure reinforcements which improve its rigidity and like the coupé version, it uses a combination of both steel and plastic composite bodywork. Powered by a 5.7 litre 275 horsepower version of the Corvette LT1, the Z28 Camaro can be equipped with either a T56 Borg Warner six-speed manual transmission or the optional 4L60-E four-speed automatic. ABS brakes and dual air-bags are also part of standard safety features

**Right**

The California Camaro is another of the mind-expanding concept cars from Chevrolet. This new design was one of the first products from Chevrolet's Advanced Styling Studio in Santa Barbara, California. Most concept cars are built out of glassfibre, but this wild new shape was stamped out of steel in a project to advance the designer's knowledge of building advanced creations using real-time methods. Based around a 2+2 interior layout, the coupé incorporates fully flush glass with vertically opening doors. The California Camaro project is fully functional and features a dual overhead cam V6, rear drive and MacPherson strut suspensions at all four corners. It's not what the current generation Camaro looks like, but the details prove that it's possible to build new shapes never before attempted using traditional engineering methods

The latest generation of Camaros has been five years in development. It retains all the sporty features which have made the Camaro so popular for so long: front engine-rear drive, V8 power and slick coupé styling. Its new lines can be seen in the shapes that were penned for the California Camaro concept car. Inside it can carry five but four in more comfort. It ranges from a base model with a V6 on up to the 300 hp LT1 Corvette engine option for tyre-frying performance. Air bag and ABS make it the safest Camaro ever built and its wild new lines make it the best looking Chevy for the early nineties

**Above**

*For those who prefer coupés over sedans, Pontiac has the Grand Am GT two-door. The stylishly rounded body features the trademark split Pontiac grille wrapped into a shape which delivers a low .34 Cd. The sporty styling of the Grand Am make this car a winner, especially when equipped with the 180 bhp Quad 4 engine. The all-aluminum Quad 4 engine makes a rousing rush for the red line with a multitude of mechanical sounds that yell performance. The Grand Am uses a front-wheel-drive platform which has been extensively developed to deliver sure-footed handling, ride comfort and crisp steering response. Top speed of the GT is 125 mph and 0-60 mph can be ticked off in 8.2 seconds*

**Left**

*The Pontiac Grand Am sedan has more than enough performance to back up its aggressive looks. With either the 180 bhp DOHC 16-valve 2.3-litre four-cylinder Quad 4 or the 160 bhp 3.3-litre pushrod V6 engine, as this car was optioned, performance is snappy. Good ergonomics, a thick-rimmed steering wheel and supportive seats team up with the excellent front-wheel-drive handling to make the Grand Am GT into a fun sports sedan. Four doors and spacious rear seats accommodate four in comfort and five in a pinch, while standard anti-lock brakes keep everyone safe*

**Above**

*When Pontiac decided to increase the performance of the 3.8 litre V6 engine, they turned to a classic technology by utilising a Roots-type supercharger. But to increase fuel-mileage, Pontiac borrowed some modern turbocharger technology and included a wastegate. All of this adds up to 205 bhp and a stomping 260 ft/lb of torque. While all this torque is great to get the adrenals pumping, it also prohibits the use of a manual transmission which would not be able to operate reliably with these forces. Even with an automatic transmission, all of this power being applied through the front wheels would compromise grip and handling were it not for the standard traction control keeping things steady. With a supercharger, Pontiac has given the Bonneville an engine that can keep it at the front of the pack*

**Left**

*The Bonneville SSEi offers a large dose of Pontiac Excitement! With a 3.8 litre V6 motivated by a Roots-type supercharger, this car shines with plenty of performance and comfort. The stylish exterior is complemented by an attractive and convenient interior that features such wonders as a head-up display (HUD) speedometer readout and dual airbags. Despite having a full load of standard luxury features on the SSEi, Pontiac has still managed to undercut the price of BMW's baseline 5-series by nearly $10,000 while providing performance equal to, or surpassing, the upperline German models. The Bonneville SSEi demonstrates just how well Pontiac can build performance family cars*

**Above**

The Pontiac Stinger is another 'New Edge Concept' from Pontiac. This wild lime green beach buggy is designed for commuting and weekend off-road fun. Powered by an advanced, multi-valve, four- cylinder engine producing 190 hp, it makes life easy with a four- speed automatic transmission, fully independent suspension and ABS. The Stinger is designed for outdoor living with a built-in camp stove, pull-out radio, 110-volt electrical system to power appliances, a picnic mess kit and binoculars for checking out the babes on the beach. The rollbar contains a set of pop-up driving lights, and the rear seat can be raised for better off-road visibility

**Above right**

Pontiac re-defined the 2+2 idea with the Sunfire concept sports coupé. This hot-looking little four-seater features a set of unique door openings which use one-and-a-half doors on each side to facilitate access to the rear seats while allowing normal front seat entry and exit. It is powered by a front-mounted 16-valve dual overhead cam 2-litre engine that delivers 190 hp and 205 ft/lb of torque. It also features fully independent suspension, anti-lock brakes and five-speed automatic transmission. The body is hi-tech carbon fibre and uses 20-inch front wheels with 21-inch rear wheels. The interior features all the latest electronics including a HUD, or Head Up Display

**Right**

The Pontiac Protosport4 is a concept car that offers comfort for four people while providing performance and handling normally achieved only in sports cars. Pontiac have set their sights on building affordable sports cars, and the Protosport4 is the fourth generation of the latest series of hi-tech vehicles. The Protosport4 features four clamshell doors, four-wheel steering and a DOHC V8 to power a Hydra-matic four-speed automatic that feeds the rear wheels. Interestingly, this car features 19-inch front wheels and 20-inch wheels at the rear

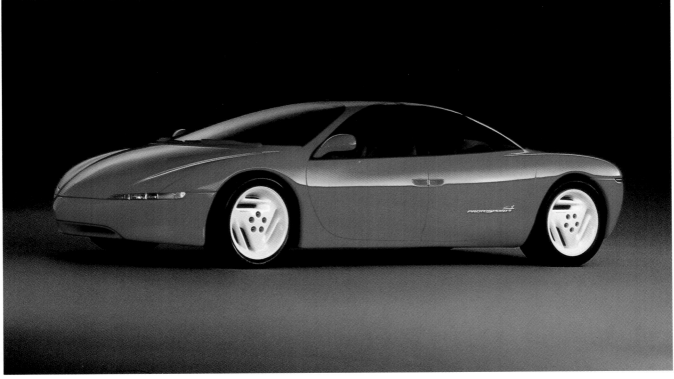

**Above**

The Pontiac Firebird has been around since the late sixties. Over the years it has mutated with the Camaro with which it has always shared its platform and some sheet metal. Still built as a convertible and a coupé, the Firebird is sold under the GTA, Formula and Trans Am name tags. The Formula featured here comes with the high-output 5.0 litre PFI V8 and a five-speed manual transmission. The Formula also comes with the WS6 sports suspension which gives the Firebird a wonderful sporty edge that sets it hard and fast for back country touring. The 5.7 litre/ 350 cubic inch V8 is optional on only the GTA Firebird, and comes only with a four-speed automatic transmission. In either form, the Firebird has been a mind-blower on the both the street and track

**Right**

The latest generation of Pontiac Firebirds is now on the showroom floor. More than five years in the making, the new Firebird displays distinct breeding from the Pontiac Banshee show car with its wide, round nose and roll-around glass. The Firebird continues to share the same platform as Chevrolet's Camaro, but the Firebird has been engineered as a distinct model unto itself. In its best years the Firebird Trans Am sold more than 100,000 units, and Pontiac are hoping for a return to the profit-earning years. Power delivery starts with a V6 and can be rolled right on up to the 300 hp LT1 V8 sourced from the Corvette. It's sure to earn a place in the hearts of performance lovers. Its slick lines and performance potential make it a hot ticket for the nineties

**Above**

*The Salsa is aimed squarely at the young and the young at heart. Pontiac conceived it as their seventh nineties concept vehicle. It can be built as either a convertible, panel delivery van or as an all-weather hatchback for hauling mountain bikes or surfboards. Based around a central unit, any of the body combinations can be added to the stock frame assembly. Its 'widetrack' stance gives it exceptional stability with the roominess of a full-sized family sedan. It was conceived under the direction of Terry Henline, the Director of General Motors Advanced Concept Center as a five seater to suit the warm weather climates. Underneath it features a unique semi-twist-axle suspension with stamped control arms. Power to the front-drive transaxle is supplied by an experimental 1.5 litre double overhead cam four-cylinder engine*

**Right**

*The Firebird is known for its tyre-frying performance. We just wanted to make sure you got to see it in action!*

**Above**

Pontiac's wild Banshee proves that American designers can set a standard for automotive design. Its curvaceous forms flow into an aerodynamic body that show the potential styles of American-built supercars of the future. The Banshee was used as a prop in the movie Back to the Future – III (look for it cruising by in a side street). The Banshee could well be the Firebird of the future, available from a Pontiac dealer in your neighbourhood around, shall we say, 1998

**Right**

The Banshee's sharply pointed nose and huge glass area give the advanced coupé an air of speed just sitting still. I drove this car at Watkins Glen Raceway just after it was built, and I was amazed at how much of a superb view the passengers get from their leather- covered bucket seats. Inside the Banshee, it is decked out with TV rear-vision, satellite navigation and the complete whiz-bang of computer controls. It is powered by a front-mounted V8 which was especially developed for the project. It uses a one-piece block and head design and produces 230 hp

**Left**

When Pontiac and Gale Banks decided to 'go for the gold' at the Bonneville Salt Flats, they built a red Firebird with the ambition to run into the 300-mph zone and the record books. With Gale Banks building the 1600 hp big-block twin-turbo Pontiac, the car was shipped to Bonneville for testing. It ran in the 290-mph zone on two occasions, but on the third try, with Don Stringfellow at the wheel, it rolled through the 300-mph barrier like a freight train heading East to set a new Land Speed Record

**Above**

When Buick redesigned the Park Avenue line, they decided to drop a bombshell by creating a new sporty persona for their luxury family sedan. Titled the Ultra, it comes with the same snappy 3.8 litre supercharged V6 engine that powers the Pontiac Bonneville SSEi and Oldsmobile Touring Sedan. Rated at 205 hp, the V6 offers smooth power delivery and handling to match. Underneath it features a Touring Suspension, 16-inch wheels and anti-lock brakes which combine to produce a fine blend of ride and handling. Acceleration is brisk with 8.7 seconds for 0-60 mph and a top speed of more than 125 mph. Inside, the Ultra features a spacious all-new interior with analog gauges and leather-cloth seats

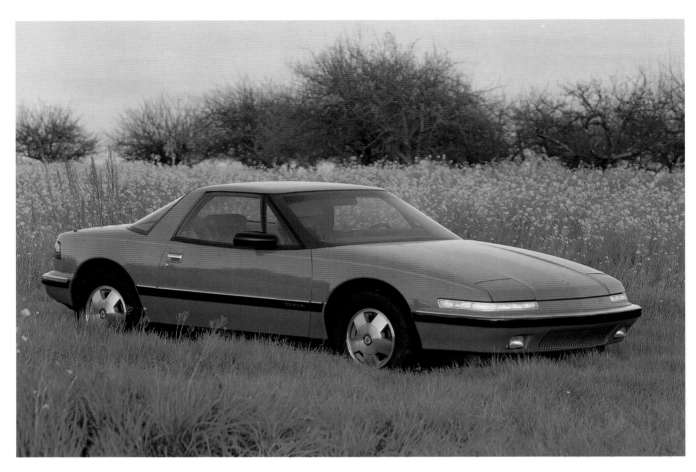

With the Reatta coupé, Buick entered the luxury two-seater market back in 1988.
Built on a shortened version of the front-wheel-drive Riviera chassis, it shared the same
3.8 litre engine. The V6 offers lively acceleration with 165 bhp and 210 ft/lb of torque.
Goodyear steel-belted radials mounted on 15-inch alloy wheels were combined with
anti-lock disc brakes to provide performance handling and braking. Luxury is first-rate
with standard leather interior, six-way adjustable bucket seats and keyless door entry.
With its impressive list of hardware and beautiful exterior sheet metal, it is surprising
that the Reatta did not meet sales expectations and was unfortunately recently
dropped from the Buick line

The Buick Riviera is a traditional American luxury coupé built in small numbers for a select market. The 170-hp V6 offers a high level of performance, while the optional Gran Sport package improves handling immensely. The Buick Riviera has a long list of standard equipment and offers good performance while offering seating for four

**Above left**

*Buick designed the Lucerne concept car in 1986 to show where Buicks were headed in the future. One of the goals was that 'it should look like a Buick from blocks away'. Built on a lengthened Riviera chassis, it incorporates the standard 165-hp V6 mated to an electronic four-speed automatic transmission. The front-wheel-drive chassis is four-wheel independently sprung and features an anti-lock braking system. Other advanced features include computer navigation with a colour display, individual air-conditioning controls for each seat and provisions for a mobile computer. With the Lucerne concept car, Buick has given us all a glimpse of what to expect from the not-too-distant future*

**Left**

*Buick's Bolero is another advanced vehicle from their long list of current show cars. 'Advanced' is the key word for this car with its 3.3-litre supercharged engine and extensive use of fibre optics. The 'force-fed' V6 produces 206 hp which drives the front wheels through an electronic four-speed automatic transmission. Anti-lock brakes are provided for straight and safe stops. Lighting for the instrument panel, doors, controls and tail lights is handled by fibre optics using a central light source. Uniform lighting and ease of maintenance are two of the benefits provided by this technology.*

**Above**

*The Essence is Buick's show car for its full-size sedan line, the Park Avenue. The attractive and aerodynamic body was designed to convey a futuristic yet distinctively Buick shape while still offering practicality for possible production. To provide a realistic future powerplant, Buick chose to increase power over the present V6 engine by modifying the heads, manifold, and injection so it now delivers a total of 185 hp which would give the Essence the capacity to accelerate to 60 mph in nine seconds*

**Above**

Buick are searching for the perfect car of the future. The Sceptre concept car is one of those stepping stones to the future. They chose to redefine what an advanced five-passenger rear-drive sedan should look like and how it should drive. From its traditional Buick touch with the grille to its non-traditional body shapes, the Sceptre's slick architecture offers aggressive style with 280 hp of supercharged V6 power, traction control, luxury leather interior and computer-controlled sports suspension

**Right**

Buick Wildcat's engine is a mid-mounted 231 cubic inch/3.8 litre V6 which features four-valves per cylinder, twin cams per bank and sequential Cross-Fire Fuel Injection. Its dyno figures deliver 230 hp at 6000 rpm with 245 ft/lb of torque. The fuel injection is programmable so it can be 'tuned' on the road from the driver's seat

**Overleaf**

The Buick Wildcat was done as a one-off so the engineering department could exercise their talents on something exciting and fast. David P Rand designed it as a Corvette-like sports coupé, and the Wildcat carries off the design theme using one of the first 'cab-forward' designs which have now become the trend in nineties' automotive styling. In profile the Wildcat looks like it's going the other way, but from the front you know it's coming your way and more than likely very quickly. The Wildcat was built as a fully functional two-seat sports coupé powered by an advanced V6. All-up weight is less than 3000 lb (1300 kg) and its V6 power delivers a power-to-weight ratio of 13:1

**Above left**

the '95 Oldsmobile Aurora sedan is being pitched up against the best German sports sedans. Powered by a downsize 4.0 litre Northstar V8 from the Cadillac division. The DOHC, 32-valve Aurora V8 produces a beefy 250 horsepower and delivers its muscle through an advanced electronically controlled, four-speed Hydra-Matic 4T80-E transmission to the front wheels. Its power curve is designed to offer excellent mid-range power response. It rides on fully-independent suspension which firmly plants its 16 inch alloy wheels on the pavement. Safety features include ABS brakes, air-bags and hi-tech side-impact engineering. The body styling is aggressive and sensuous with tightly wrapped sheet metal, no-grille and stubby tail with full-width tail lights

**Left**

The Saturn SC2 coupé is the hottest model from General Motors new Saturn division. General Motors wanted to create a product line which could compete head-on with not only European but Asian competition. They created Saturn to build a new line of compact automobiles. Assembled using mostly plastic body panels, Saturn offers the SC2 coupé as its top of the line sports model. The Sc2 is powered by a 124 horsepower, dual-cam 1.9 litre all-aluminium engine driving the front wheels. The SC2 comes equipped with Traction Control, air-bag and anti-lock

brakes as standard and offers responsive handling and nippy performance at a price which has brought buyers flooding into Saturn dealerships

**Above**

With the trend started by the British Range Rover, luxury sports utility vehicles have managed to seize a large portion of the American market. While they started off as rugged and uncomfortable vehicles more at home off the road than on it, they have evolved into luxurious automobiles that can be found in such locales as Rodeo Drive. With their increase in popularity, so did the numbers of manufacturers, until even Oldsmobile has one. The Bravada combines a powerful engine, a luxurious interior and off-road ruggedness to provide a spectacular package. With the optional high-performance 4.3-litre engine producing 200 hp, the Bravado is a real screamer and has plenty of torque to pull you over even the steepest hills. The optional leather interior is of the finest material available on any GM product and can make even long trips more pleasant. The Bravada is an excellent vehicle that challenges the Range Rover head-on

**Above**

The Oldsmobile Trofeo Coupe is the ultimate in personal four-seaters from Olds. Its rounded 'aero' lines, hidden headlights, huge 16-inch wheels and sci-fi looks give the Trofeo a presence all of its own. Built in small numbers, this $25,000 coupé is powered by a 170-hp version of the generic GM V6. Based on the Oldsmobile Toronado, the Trofeo offers FE3 sports touring suspension, luxurious leather interior, special body cladding and colours. It also comes with anti-lock brakes

**Right**

Oldsmobile would never have built a car like this unless the Europeans had sold them so successfully in the States. Audi, BMW and Mercedes-Benz all showed the way with luxury touring sedans that combined power, handling and ride with a luxury interior. The Oldsmobile Ninety-Eight Supercharged Touring Sedan sets a new style with its round frontal shapes and slick bodywork. Powered by the same engine used in the Pontiac Bonneville SSEi, this 3.8 litre supercharged V6 has 205 horses to lead the charge. A four-speed electronically controlled automatic transmission moves the power to the front wheels. Underneath, the FE3 sports suspension delivers an amazingly confident handling package for a front-drive sedan, while the interior treatments offer a sophisticated and comfortable environment for high speed travel

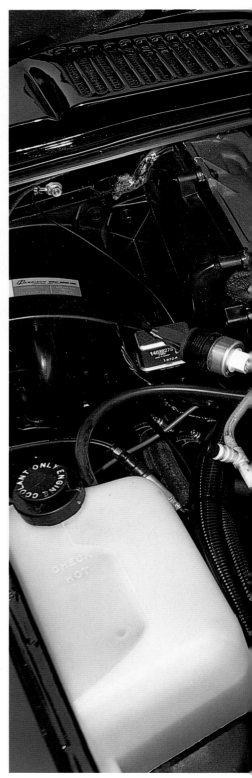

**Above**

The GMC Typhoon is a sports car built as a wagon. Hidden under its suburban-hauler bodywork is a road blaster that can peel the skin off a Ferrari 348ts, stomp on a 911 SC and run with a Corvette. Sounds too weird to be true? It's not. The Typhoon comes with all-wheel-drive, adhesive-like handling, ABS and a 285-hp turbocharged, inter-cooled V6. Based on the 4.3-litre Vortec V6, the power train for the Typhoon is identical to the Syclone truck, also from GMC. Both are a result of GMC trucks' pursuit of the sports truck market, and both are wildly fast. It's the type of 'Q-ship' that we all dream of. The Typhoon can blow off anything that rolls up beside it at the lights in the wink of an eye. Standstill to 60 mph comes whacking up in 5.3 seconds. While the top speed is only 124 mph, which isn't that quick because of a fuel computer cut-off, when you can go from 0-100 mph in 16 seconds flat, you know you're truly truckin'

**Right**

The turbocharged V6 Syclone engine is in many respects very conventional, with cast iron block and heads. At this point it all changes. Add a Mitsubishi RH06 turbo, intercooler, 8.4:1 compression, electronic fuel injection and an electronic engine management system and you get 285 hp and an amazing 360 ft/lb of torque, making this engine the master blaster of the V6 set

**Above**

When GMC Trucks entered the truck performance stakes they decided that they should set a Land Speed Record as part of the programme. They built this slick Sonoma extended-cab into a 500 hp, turboed/V6 race car and went to Bonneville. They came home with a record for a closed coupé of 196 mph. The project so excited them that within the year they released a street version called the Syclone, an all-wheel-drive turbo/V6 super truck

**Right**

GMC had hoped for a 200 mph record when they first went to the salt. They knew that they could be the first truck through the barrier so they returned with this revised version to try again. With Don Stringfellow at the wheel once again, the truck pulled a two-way FIA record run of 204 mph to up their own record and be the 'Top Gun' trucker at Bonneville. Again the truck was powered by a race-prepared Vortec V6 street motor, running twin turbos, inter-coolers, water-chilling and fuel injection which all helped produce more than 500 hp

**Above**

Geo is the import division of Chevrolet. It offers products from three manufacturers under the Geo title. One of the most popular vehices is the Geo Tracker, a mini 4x4. This trick concept Tracker is set for cruising to the beach or tearing up the dunes. Either way it's got to be a cool way to travel

**Left**

Another concept for the Geo Tracker is this 'Street Racer' built for Geo by a Southern California hot rod shop. All decked out in candy purple and yellow graphics, this ground-hugging new age hot rod is ready for some hot laps on cruise night

**Above**

The Ultralite's interior is spacy and efficient. The dash features a huge backlit speedo with all the other controls falling right to hand or finger. The steering wheel contains an air bag and the controls for the sound system. The four-place interior is surprisingly roomy, as the narrow 18-inch wheels do not intrude into the foot wells of the rear seat as they do in many contemporary automobiles

**Left**

GM's Ultralite is a car of the future aimed at showing the public that the future of the low-polluting/high fuel efficiency vehicle is not in dull looks. Designed to deliver 100 mpg or better, the Ultralite concept car produced a stunning .192 Cd in the wind tunnel which is exceptional for a vehicle of this size. It offers the interior space of a large sedan, while its overall length is that of a mid-sized Mazda. The body and chassis are built as a tub of composite carbon fibre from which a steel space frame is hung for the power unit and suspension. Power is supplied by a rear-mounted 111 hp two-stroke using the latest direct-injection. The combination of features allows the Ultralite to travel through the air at 55 mph on 4 hp, compared to 15 hp for a contemporary mid-size sedan

# CHRYSLER

Since the heyday of the muscle car in the late sixties, Chrysler has been consistently ranked the number three Detroit builder by the automotive industry. The 'gas wars' of the early seventies nearly crushed the company because it produced 'heavy metal' with big cubic inches. But from a near knock-out position it has bounced back with amazing vigour with Lee A Iacocca at the helm. This return to a position of strength has come about because of good management and a new understanding of what the public expected from their automobiles. The timely introduction of the first minivan got their sales moving back up the charts. Even the performance freaks weren't forgotten – Carroll Shelby was brought into the fold to help guide Chrysler into the nineties with some new sporty cars. The Dodge Daytona coupés were soon reworked Shelby versions which offered turbo power and high performance handling. Even the seemingly sluggish little Omni econo-car was transformed into one of the hottest tickets by Shelby when it became the Omni GLH powered by a 2.2 litre, 150 hp turbo motor with matching high performance suspension. This pocket-rocket got Chrysler some of its best press since the minivan. The design teams moved into new territory with a broader range of Chryslers, Dodges and Plymouths, all based on the same front-wheel-drive platform. Chrysler added Eagle to the company line up when they absorbed American Motors in the late eighties. Other ventures have also spawned fresh products. The new Laser/Talon is based on a co-operative venture with Mitsubishi, who build it for Chrysler in the United States. The nineties also brought with them the Dodge Stealth, another co-operative project with Mitsubishi. This time the real meaning of high-performance was given a new perspective with a line of Corvette-sized coupés which offer 'slap you in the ears' performance with options including 300 hp twin-turbo V6 power, 4x4 and seating for four. But the most exciting news was left for 1993 with the introduction of the Viper V10 'retro-rocket'. This exotic and aggressively powerful roadster took the Detroit Auto Show by

*Dodge's remarkable 'Retro-rocket', the Viper, is here. Dodge revealed their Cobra-killer at the Detroit Auto Show in 1989, where the reaction from the press and public was ecstatic. Moving quickly, Chrysler took advantage of the plaudits the Viper received to announce that it would be built. Using a small and highly motivated staff, they turned the dream into a driving reality in less than two years. Powered by a 488 cubic inch V10, the Viper draws on all of the nostalgia of the Cobra for its style and feel while still using the technology of the nineties*

storm back in 1989; within a short time Chrysler had decided that it would follow the same destiny as the Corvette and go from 'show-car to street-car'. Again, Carroll Shelby was a motivating force working for Chrysler as a consultant on this project. Chrysler's rocky road back to prominence as a manufacturer has been a long and arduous journey. Its stunning new LH sedans have hit the showroom floors. Judging from our first drive impressions, Ford and GM had better take note that Chrysler is back with a vengeance, building vehicles which scream performance, luxury and fun out loud.

**Above**

*The Viper's GTS Coupé is a 'retro' sixties racer. The blue and white livery and sidepipes scream Grand Sport Corvette to anyone with half a memory. Built as a concept car for the LA Auto Show, the Viper GTS is powered by the production V10 but rolls on trick, five-spoke 17-inch wheels carrying 275 and 335 mm tyres front and rear respectively. This impressive amount of rubber teamed up with an all-independent suspension is designed to deliver a tenacious grip on the skid pad*

**Right**

*With the 1992 production run already sold out, orders were being taken for the 1993 models in early 1992. The suggested dealer price is about US $55,000, but the first 200 moved at much higher prices. Each of these buyers were willing to pay a premium to have their share of excitement, provided by a 400 hp motor housed in a body with lines so exotic they're almost obscene. Part of the plan to make the Viper a 'real' sports car included not weighing down the car with 'useless' luxuries. This theme is carried off in the interior, where no air conditioning or even roll-up windows are offered*

**Above**

To create horsepower in a quantity worthy of a true Cobra successor, Chrysler had to combine new with old. The old is cubic inches, 488 to be exact. The new is provided by a V10 borrowed from the Dodge truck bin. But this one is cast in aluminum with a 9.1:1 compression ratio, which produces 400 hp and 450 ft/lb of torque. With the induction system sitting like a bed of snakes between the heads, the port fuel injection enables the Viper to manage almost 20 mpg on the highway. But when the hammer drops and fuel economy is forgotten, the Viper will scream from 0-60 mph in only 4.6 seconds and run on 'til the 159 mph top-speed is attained

**Right**

A real snake charmer was required to make the Viper truly deadly. Carroll Shelby himself brought some of his thinking and classic magic to help promote the Viper. Shelby's influence helped to keep the bean-counters at Chrysler from diluting the production car into something tame like the ZR-1. Tame, this car is not: the quarter mile can be torn apart in 13.2 seconds at 107 mph, soundly beating the ZR-1 and showing that at heart it's a true snake!

**Above**

The IROC Daytonas are the production version of the car used for the International Race Of Champions. In this series the best drivers in the world are pitted against each other in identical cars prepared for racing. Because everything down to the mechanics are equal, only skill determines the winner. Although the race-prepped versions are rear-wheel-drive V8 cars, versus the IROC R/T front-wheel-drive 2.2 litre turbo four-cylinder, the production version offers plenty of go. With 224 hp powering this lightweight chassis, performance is spectacular. Sixteen-inch wheels help the IROC package get the horses to the ground and promote excellent handling

**Right**

The Plymouth Prowler concept roadster is another great idea from Chrysler. Its 'retro' hot rod style is greener than you would expect, with a 240 hp high-output V6, driving a four-speed rear-mounted transaxle. The Prowler rides on a custom alloy chassis and features a hand-formed aluminium body, retaining, as with quite a few of the machines in this book, design cues from earlier cars from the company stable. Interestingly, the Prowler meets all current safety standards, with dual air bags, acceptable bumpers and lighting

**Left**

The Plymouth Slingshot was designed and built as a two-seat sports car of the future as part of a project between the Art Center School of Design students and the Design Staff at Chrysler. It incorporates motorcycle concepts and promotes the 'small is good' thinking that Chrysler is looking to build in the future. It uses a rigid carbon fibre tub and is powered by a 2.2 litre twin-cam, turbo, four-cylinder engine. The engine sits across the Slingshot sideways behind the cabin. Access is gained to the interior via a lift-up roof section which tilts forward for entry and exit

**Above**

The Eagle Talon TSi AWD is one of the snappiest and most adhesive small sports coupés in the world. Built in Normal, Illinois, at the Diamond Star assembly plant, the Talon is the product of the cooperative venture between Mitsubishi and Chrysler at Diamond Star. Powered by a 2.0 litre turbocharged and intercooled four-cylinder engine that develops 195 hp, the TSi All-Wheel-Drive is one rad road-burner. A five-speed trans-axle normally takes care of shifting but a four-speed automatic is also available. The Talon's stylish lines wrap down into colour-matched bumpers and side moldings

**Above left**

The Dodge Stealth was Chrysler's first venture into the modern supercar league. Even if you can't read a book by the cover, you can probably guess that the Stealth is fast just by looking at the aggressive body styling – power from a 300 hp twin-turbo V6. This mass of power is put down to the road via an all-wheel-drive system which makes this 2+2 sports coupé a screamer. Acceleration to 60 mph is in the low five-second range, and the top speed of more than 150 mph is quickly reached. The AWD and 245 mm tyres mounted on 17-inch wheels offer a huge 'foot print' of rubber

**Left**

The Eagle Talon has more to offer than just straight-line performance. The suspension has been race-proven and developed so the AWD can keep the four patches of rubber cemented to the ground. The P205/55VR radials ride on 16-inch alloy wheels, while braking is provided by the optional ABS fitted with 10-inch discs in front and 10.32-inch discs in the rear. With all the right hardware and extensive development, the Eagle Talon TSi has become a true high-performance sports car. And check out that stud behind the wheel! Future race material for sure

**Above**

Chrysler's hot new mini-car, the Neon, will hit the streets in '94 as a four-door, five-seater with a two-door coupé to follow. The Neon's curvaceous lines include stylish oval headlights and plenty of glass. Its Cab-Forward style follows Chrysler's LH design themes, pushing the wheels out to the corners of the body which produces an amazing improvement in interior space. The Neon offers 'European handling' comparable with any of the mini-sports sedans from across the pond, but with the added benefit of dual airbags and a full five-passenger interior. The base engine is a 16-valve single OHC 132 horsepower four-cylinder while the sports engine is a DOHC unit developing around 160 horsepower

The Chrysler Thunderbolt concept coupé is a nineties vision of the stunning
Thunderbolt dream car the company built in the 1940s. The new coupé is styled using
Chrysler cab-forward thinking to carry four and is powered by a 4-litre, 32-valve
DOHC all-aluminium V8 rated at 270 hp. The car is fully driveable and the aggressive
styling is allied to traction control, ABS brakes and all-wheel independent suspension

*The Chrysler Cirrus Concept car once again stamped the cab-forward idea into another prototype vehicle. This slick front engine family sports sedan of the future uses super-wide angle door openings for easy four-passenger access. Virtually no straight lines appear in the body work, with a rounded turret, oval shaped front and rear glass and wheels set at near-extreme corners of the chassis*

**Above**

The Chrysler 300 Concept Car followed the Viper sports roadster onto the show circuit. The boys at Chrysler's Design Studios took the powerful V10 engine and suspension from the Viper and built a fully functional four-door, four passenger super-sedan in the 300. With the amazing success of the Viper, Chrysler are considering a limited production run for the 300 in 1994

**Left**

It may seem strange to put a Jeep into a performance car book, but with the way our view of performance has changed in the last few years, vehicles like the Jeep Grand Cherokee and Grand Wagoneer offer as much and better handling and performance than some sporty cars. Jeeps like the Grand Cherokee are making forays into new areas. While tackling mountains as usual, the new Jeep is out to conquer sports sedans. The Grand Cherokee offers the most aerodynamic body of any sports/utility vehicle as well as the first with a standard driver's side air-bag and anti-lock brakes. Standard leather seats and full complement of other features combine to make luxury first-class. The 4.0 litre, six-cylinder is rated at a strong 190 hp and for true performance fans an optional 5.2 litre V8 is offered. A highly developed suspension with coil-springs at all corners combines with optional P225/70R15 radials to make handling just as good on-road as it is off-road

**Left**

Sports sedans are one of the most exciting sectors of the current car market in the US. We have the Corvette, the Mustang, the Camaro and the Viper but in reality they are only 'dream cars' for most folks. But sports sedans which can carry five passengers at speed and in comfort are highly sought after. Chrysler's new 'cab forward-look' Dodge Intrepid ES has just hit the market powered by a 214 hp V6 and rolling on a well-tuned sports suspension. The ES comes with all the bits and pieces which blend performance and luxury into one package. The interior has a fine readable analog dash and the seating is leather faced and extremely comfortable

**Above**

The LH Chrysler sports sedans are sold under three different titles, and this Eagle Vision STi version is the best-looking of three very pretty cars. Fully independent suspension is mounted at the corners of a chassis that utilises Chrysler's unique 'cab forward' design concept. In keeping with its sporty pretensions the Vision TSi is a stable, luxurious and high speed touring machine. The powerplant is the work of Howard Padgham's engine team at Chrysler. This group developed a strong and interesting high performance 3.5 litre, two-cam, 24-valve V6 for the LH. It is rated at 214 hp at 6000 rpm and comes home with a wide (221 ft/lb) torque band induced by using a special dual plane induction manifold for the fuel injection. Prices run US $15,000 to US $25,000

**Above**

The Plymouth Duster was re-introduced mid-year 1992 as a performance version of the compact Sundance. The Duster is fitted with a standard SOHC V6 and a five-speed trans-axle driving the front wheels. The exterior styling is updated with gold Duster graphics, monochromatic trim and a rear spoiler. Riding on either 15 × 6 steel wheels or optional aluminum wheels, the suspension is fitted with stabiliser bars front and rear, and an optional ABS controls the 10.18-inch discs in front and 10.57-inch in the rear. It's a hot little ride that has proven to be a winner with 'the young and the restless'

**Right**

The sporty new Chrysler LHS is aimed right at the pocketbook of the bay boomer BMW/Lexus buyer. The LHS offers a mass of comfort and luxury features mixed with a good lashing of drivability from its front drive, independent suspended, cab-forward platform. Powered by a 214 hp 3.5 litre V6 which features four-valve, twin-cam heads and dual-phase tuned fuel injection, power is transferred via a four-speed automatic transaxle. The combination marches right along, dashing off a respectable 0 to 60 mph in just nine seconds. Stock ABS brakes and the Traction Control function of the final drive, help to promote a feeling of driver security. Chrysler have finally done what the Europeans have been doing for years—mixing luxury, style and performance into a family sedan—but in a way only Detroit is still able to do, affordably

**Above**

*As the last in a line of show cars that led to Chrysler's new LH sedans, the Eagle Optima is the most developed prototype. In person the Optima is one of the finest looking family sports sedans ever to hit the show circuit. This is a near fully functional cab forward design and is fitted with an all-aluminum 4.0 litre 32-valve V8 designed specifically to drive the front wheels. Tom Gale, Chrysler's Design Chief, was in charge of styling which is contemporary, attractive and unique. Although the Optima is quite close to the production LH, the production version is fitted with a hi-tech V6 in lieu of the V8*

**Right**

*The Plymouth Laser is the sister car to the Eagle Talon TSi. Built alongside each other, they share the same 195 hp Diamond Star engine and optional AWD system. The performance matches the Talon and based on value-for-money performance the Laser is an exceptional automobile. While they share the same body, exterior trim they have different spoilers, options and trim*

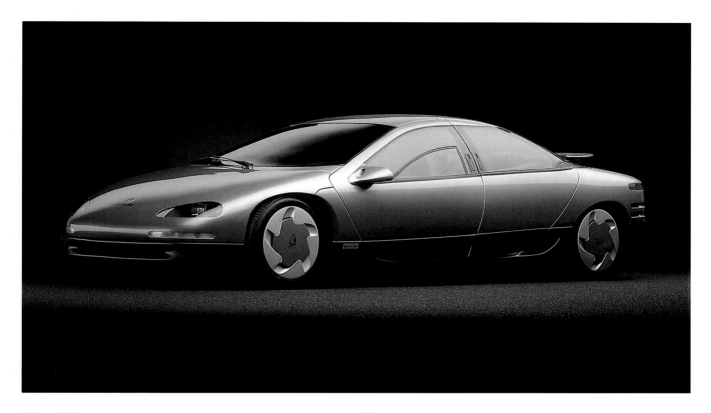

**Above left**

*If your passion runs towards small, fast, and fun cars, then the Plymouth Speedster was made for you. It is a one-off prototype built at Chrysler's Pacifica Design Center in Carlsbad, California. The slick Speedster design utilises motorcycle componentry to keep the vehicle compact. Although the car has no top, it has a protective roll-over hoop similar to its big brother's, the Viper. Its huge wheels are painted fluorescent green to contrast the black exterior and yellow interior*

**Left**

*The interior of the Plymouth Speedster is where the motorcycle influence is most evident. Aircraft-like controls are provided in lieu of a conventional wheel and controls. Even the steering column is styled to liken the forks on a motorcycle. Despite having motorcycle-like qualities, the Speedster provides for passenger safety with four-point racing seat belts. Overall the Plymouth Speedster looks like 50 per cent motorcycle, 50 per cent car and 100 per cent fun!*

**Above**

*The Portofino show car combines the best of Lamborghini and Chrysler. Styled by Chrysler's Tom Gale, the Portofino makes use of the Lamborghini Jalpa's mid-engine running gear by utilising a cab forward design on a long wheelbase. The 3.5 litre V8 engine produces 247 hp that it feeds through the five-speed trans-axle. Because the Portofino was built on an existing car, build-time was sped up immensely. Although designed exclusively by Chrysler it uses some Lamborghini styling cues, such as the clamshell doors. The Portofino has won much public acclaim including best of show at the Detroit auto show*

# FORD

Henry Ford didn't invent the automobile as much as it may seem from some history books. Henry simply took a good idea and made it better. His heirs have carried on that tradition virtually without fault ever since. What caused Ford vehicles to be so popular was that they were simple and reliable. But they also offered 'snappy' performance with some of the first mass-production V8 power.

The not-too-distant past of Ford performance includes the introduction of the Thunderbird in the mid fifties to compete with the Corvette, and in the following decade the introduction of one of Ford's most successful performance products, the Mustang. During the sixties and seventies Ford took the World Sports Car championship, beat Ferrari at Le Mans, were NHRA Super Stock drag racing champs, won Indy and made the Mustang a winner with the Sports Car Club of America Trans Am racing. Shelby built his Mustang muscle cars during these years which also added considerably to Ford's performance image. But the seventies also produced a series of low performance economy models which were built in response to the 1973 oil crisis.

The eighties brought renewed interest in street performance by all the divisions at Ford. The Mustang got a V8 again, the Thunderbird went Turbo with a forced induction four-cylinder developing 145 hp backed up to a sports handling package. Then it was completely revised in '88 with a powerful 210 hp supercharged V6, IRS rear suspension and gracious bodywork. The '93 Mustang in its GT form is a 'master-blaster', but after thirteen years using basically the same platform, Ford are currently designing and testing a whole new Mustang line-up. Even Lincoln have got into the act with a real 'Hot Rod Lincoln', the fabulous '93 Mark VIII. The sign of the blue oval has become a measure with which to gauge street performance. The success of the Mustang GT, the Mark VIII and the new Ford Probe are markers for all in the industry for both longevity and performance.

*Driving the Mustang LX 5.0L convertible is one of the best ways to get a tan. With the top down and the GT's high-performance engine and suspension underfoot, becoming bronze has never been easier. Although handling is brisk, the suspension is not overly stiff. Included in the 5.0 litre package are power lumbar sport seats and a leather-wrapped steering wheel to make this ride even better*

The Mustang Mach III concept car is a wild idea for a two-seat roadster. The 'Hot Poppy' red Mach III is powered by a supercharged version of the alloy 4.6 litre V8. This engine is from the Lincoln Mark VIII coupé and is designed to run on either methanol or gasoline. Power to the rear wheels is via a six-speed manual transmission. The sweeping lines include echoes from past Mustangs which help to reinforce the Ford look while allowing an individual persona. The 19-inch chrome alloy wheels are shod with 315/40R tyres on the rear, with fat 245/45Rs at the rear. The high performance theme runs from nose to tail and includes an active aero spoiler, full electronic instrumentation – and a 1000-watt stereo

Ford created a true high-performance car out of the Thunderbird with their Super Coupé version. Powered by a supercharged V6 which delivers 210 hp to the rear wheels through a standard five- speed manual transmission, the SC runs head to head with the Mustang GT and the Z-28 Camaro. The Sports Coupé's sport suspension is fully independent and electronically adjustable to keep the 225/60ZR rubber stuck to the road. Side bolsters in the sport seats help to keep you in your seat when the pavement becomes twisty, and standard analog gauges, including a tachometer and boost gauge, provide the engine's vital signs. Braking is first-rate with four-wheel anti-lock discs

**Above**

*The Lincoln Mark VII Bill Blass Signature Edition is designed as a high performance luxury car. With Ford's high output 5.0 litre V8 and a standard sport suspension, the Mark VII performance goal is easily reached. The rear-wheel-drive coupé is fitted with 225/60R tyres mounted on 16-inch alloy rims. Anti-lock brakes are standard to dissipate the speed, and an air bag is fitted in case you run out of room. Luxury abounds in the cockpit, including standard leather seats, making the Mark VII a nineties blend of comfort and muscle*

**Right**

*The slick new '94 Mustang was designed by a team headed by Bud Magaldi. Available in both coupé and convertible, the new model replaces the 'Fox Mustang' originally introduced in 1979. The GT 5.0L HO SEFI V-8 version will produce in excess of 215 horsepower but later versions could include the new modular four-cam V8 engine which currently powers the Mark VIII Lincoln coupé. The suspension uses a MacPherson strut front and four-link rear end assembly. The bold new body design reflects extensive Ford research of '90s consumer taste. Ford very much wanted to retain the identity that came with the original Mustang, yet have a design that will carry them through for a good part of the next decade. A yellow GT coupé is seen here with a black V6 convertible behind*

**Left**

*The new Lincoln Mark VIII is a fine-looking luxury performer. Powered by Ford's new multi-valve V8, the Mark VIII offers fully independent suspension, luxo-cruiser interior, superb high-speed handling and a look all of its own. Lincoln have for the last ten years had a 'Hot Rod Lincoln' model in their line up, and the new nineties generation is no different. Abundant power is supplied from a 4.6 litre four-cam, 32-valve V8 developing 280 hp at 5500 rpm. This is an all-aluminum V8 running close to 10:1 compression, sequential electronic fuel injection and electronic engine management. The sweeping lines of the hood flow back into a steeply racked glass and roll off the green house into a small round trunk which still features a flirting hint of the old Continental Kit tyre molding*

**Above**

*Called 'America's Best Sports Sedan', the Taurus SHO is a rapid sedan. The SHO features a 220 hp DOHC 3.0 litre V6 that delivers 'strong-arm' acceleration that's tough enough to make a special five-speed transmission necessary to handle the stress. A revised sports suspension takes care of the abundant power providing a level of handling consistent with the SHO's sporty capabilities. The tyres are 215/60VR radials on 16-inch rims. Like any of today's good sports sedans, safety is top-notch with standard anti-lock braking and a driver's air bag. A passenger-side air bag is also optional. Interior improvements include a top-notch audio system and a leather-wrapped steering wheel*

**Above**

*The Lincoln Marque x was built as a fully functional concept car using production mechanicals from the new Mark VIII coupé. The centrepiece of this Marque x is Ford's new 4.6 Litre DOHC 280 hp production V8. But it's not all go. The snappy rounded styling gives Lincoln lovers a taste of the future. This beautiful bodywork is carefully contoured with no chrome and little trim and presents a dynamic character with its Tangerine metallic paintwork. Set up as a four-passenger sports convertible, the Marque x has a white leather interior with all the latest safety and convenience items, including rear seat entertainment centres, electronic dash and air bags*

**Left**

*The 12 intake runners of the Ford Taurus SHO engine make it one of the most impressive-looking engines ever. Looks are not deceiving as one would discover when delving into the mechanicals. A full 220 hp is created by a 3.0 litre Yamaha-built 24-valve DOHC V6. Only a manual transmission is available because Ford lacks an automatic unit strong enough to apply all the twist to the front wheels. Performance fans need not worry as the five-speed trans-axle provides strong acceleration, including a 6.6 second sprint to 60 mph*

**Above**

Even with a standard Traction-Lok rear axle, Mustang GT's have no problem lighting up their beefy high-performance rubber. Technology has actually improved the breed rather than hindered it, as seemed likely when such equipment as catalytic converters were first introduced. The high levels of performance found in the latest cars are a match for even the quickest of the classic Mustangs

**Above right**

Ford's new F-Series trucks include this snappy new hot rod F-150 'Lightning'. Developed by Ford's SVT team to highlight their move to sportier trucks, the Lightning is now a limited-production vehicle in the showroom. It has a superb handling platform with lowered suspension, dual sway bars and 17-inch cast alloy wheels shod with Firehawk GTA radials. It is powered by a hearty 240 hp 5.8 litre V8 engine

**Right**

The Ford Ranger Splash is the production "Splash" sports utility model for '93. This hot looking and fast driving mini-size truck was created in reaction to the huge resurgence of interest in trucks as sports vehicles. While not as wild as the Splash Concept Sports Utility Vehicle, the Ranger Splash is spiffy looking with its flared pick-up box made of moulded glass-filled fibreglass fenders. The Ranger Splash comes with a sports-tuned suspension which was developed by the Ford Truck Motorsports team in Florida. Power is supplied via an optional 160 horsepower 4.0 V6 and a five-speed stick transmission. It comes in either two- or four-wheel-drive and can be optioned up with alloy wheels, sports interior, super stereo and sports instruments. Even with its sporty edge the Splash can still haul a good load or pull the boat to the lake, which is really what we all want in a truck!

**Above**

*The Contour showcar is a stunning-looking vehicle. It encapsulates a mass of advanced thinking that centres around a T-Drive engine and transmission package which allows the designers to reduce the overall length of a vehicle but retain or gain interior space for passengers. The suspension uses a compact transverse leaf design in which the spring is used as the upper control arms of the suspension and as the stabiliser bar. Other innovations include the tiny but very powerful 'fibre-optic' headlights which use high-intensity discharge metal vapour lamps and the fixed package of dash, steering wheel and pedals which can be moved as a unit to adjust for driver height. The Contour's rounded organic lines came out of Jack Telnacks' Advanced Design Studio at Ford in Dearborn, Michigan*

**Right**

*The Ford Splash is a sports utility vehicle for the future. It was designed by four students at the Center for Creative Design in Detroit. This electric blue racer emulates the Beach Buggy concept of the sixties with its high stance and open big-diameter wheels. The concept is the only part of the Splash that is not firmly in the nineties, with extensive use of technology and modern ideas. Powered by a four-cylinder engine and incorporating a four-wheel-drive system, the Splash also has a driver-adjustable suspension for height and attitude. The interior is covered in fluorescent blue wet suit material, and the roof, rear hatch and side windows can be removed, upping the fun-factor many degrees*

**Above**

With classic and contemporary Mustangs so capable, Ford had an armful when they decided to create the highest performance Mustang ever. The '93 Mustang Cobra is just that, with a completely revised drivetrain and suspension updated using contemporary technology. Ford fit larger P245/45ZR tyres on 17 × 7.5 inch rims and revised the suspension with the help of men like Bob Bondurant and three-time F1 champion, Jackie Stewart. The upgrades include different spring rates, anti-roll bar diameters and shock absorber and bushing characteristics. Rear vented disc brakes have been added to make the braking ability comparable with that of the rest of the Cobra; (the observant will have noticed that this book - more or less - begins and ends with that magical American performance icon)

**Right**

The venerable 5.0 litre V8 is greatly enhanced for the '93 Mustang Cobra. Changes include the use of larger ports and valves, new intake manifold components and different roller rocker arms. With the increased flow matched by new fuel injectors and a revised engine control management system, the HO V8 will produce in excess of 275 hp. It sounds like time for Mustang owners to stop picking on Z-28s and go look for some Corvettes

**Above**

*The Ford Surf is a car designed primarily for fun. Aptly named, the Surf is the California beach cruiser and looks perfectly at home with a bunch of surfboards hanging out the back. Its pink paint-job and wave graphics make sure you get noticed on the way there, and four-wheel-drive helps get you home afterwards*

**Right**

*The Shockwave is one of Ford's most exciting show cars. This coupé offers a new direction in style and design which we hope will be carried into production cars. For now we can only guess at whether the Shockwave may have some meaning to a future Mustang, or perhaps as a new Corvette killer*

**Above**

It's hard to doubt the performance credentials of the Cougar XR7 or Thunderbird SC after seeing the supercharged engine. With the exposed Roots-type blower and a cast air intake, the engine yells serious horsepower. The 3.8 litre supercharged engine delivers a full 210 hp and offers an outstanding 315 ft/lb of torque fed to the rear wheels. These numbers translate into some truly impressive acceleration. Although the supercharged V6 has been replaced in the Cougar XR7 with a 5.0 litre V8, the Thunderbird SC retains the hot rodded six-cylinder

**Right**

The Cougar XR7 is a luxury performance coupé of the first order. With the standard 5.0 litre V8 and 200 hp, acceleration is strong. Also standard are four-wheel anti-lock disc brakes and a Traction-Lok rear end. Contact patch is provided by P225/60VR tyres mounted on 16-inch alloy wheels. A full set of analog gauges including a tachometer, an adjustable sport suspension and articulated sport seats make the sporting characteristics of this car shine

**Above**

The Capri is Mercury's two-seater convertible. Its compact size and willing turbocharged four-cylinder engine give the Capri a classic sports feel. The 1.6 litre engine benefits from both a turbocharger and 16 valves to produce 132 hp which is delivered through a 5-speed trans-axle to the front wheels. Tyres are P195/50VR mounted on 15 6-inch rims. Four-wheel disc brakes come standard, and a hardtop is optional

**Left**

America's hottest compact sports coupé, the Ford Probe GT, came back with all-new styling and all new power for '93. This time around a 24-valve V6 replaces the turbocharged four-cylinder of the previous GT. Rated at 2.5 litres with dual overhead cams, this V6 feeds 164 hp to the front wheels. Contact patches have been expanded with P225/50VR tyres mounted on 16-inch rims to plant the power and offer superior handling. The cockpit is designed for the driver with a 5-speed manual trans-axle and analog gauges. A tachometer lets you keep track of the engine, while the speedometer tells you just how easy it is to break the law with the merest dab of your right foot

# SPECIALTY BUILDERS

Europe has always been looked upon as the place where 'special' cars are built. But in the ever-mutating design studios, factories and brains of speed freaks, there are folks who simply want to go faster, look snappier or mix both.

Unlike the Europeans, the Americans mostly deal in cubic inches as a way to get to performance heaven. But there are a few exceptions to that cubic inch rule, and when they come out to play you had better put your Porsches away. Herb Adams' Jackrabbits and Sport-Tech have engines that run less than two litres but can accelerate from 0-60 mph in less than five seconds. Not only can they zap the numbers, they have the adhesion level of a tube of Crazy Glue which, combined, add up to a fun factor that runs them right off the scale.

But when it comes to cubic inches, no-one touches the Americans for brute horsepower. Vector's fabulous W2 through W8 series of supercars offer between 600 and 1500 hp depending upon options and country of delivery. Similarly, the Arex, powered by a 600 hp 5.7 litre Gale Banks twin-turbo V8, is the perfect two-seat street racer and canyon runner. Its wild lines and body-hugging interior all blend into one of the most unusual sports cars of modern times and possibly the lowest power-to-weight ratios ever built into a street car.

Others have their day in the sun, too. Advanced Concepts turned out the 'Festiva from Hell' when they assembled, in traditional fashion, a modern mutant hot rod. In the back seat they stuffed a 220 hp Ford SHO 24-valve DOHC V6. The result is a car that takes your breath away under hard acceleration.

In Florida, Consulier build their GTP 'street racer' sports coupé. This mid-engine road rocket has only been in production for two years, but it has already won a number of road racing events and challenges. Power comes from a turboed 2.2 litre Chrysler four-cylinder engine.

*The 'New-stalgia' Kurtis Craft 500 S street roadster is built to order by Jon Ward from Alpine, Texas, an enthusiast for the performance of an earlier age, using the technology of today. This roadster is a replica of a car produced by one of America's great racing car builders of the 1950s, Frank Kurtis. Kurtis won the Indy 500 five times (1950-55), and exploited that experience to stretch one of his Indy Roadsters into this two-seat street roadster. He has built a production run of 500 S replicas, powered by 308 ci Chevrolet V8s, producing 530 horsepower. With his wife navigating, he won the Mexican road race 'La Carrera Panamericana' in 1991, with another Kurtis 500 S replica placed second. His greatest triumph, and for $69,000, you can have a road version of your own*

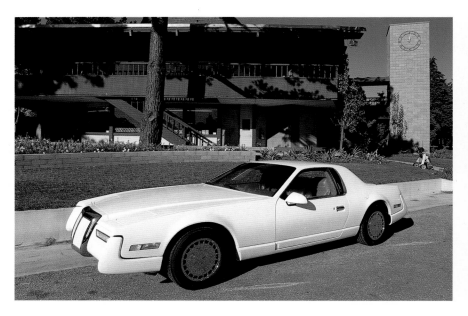

**Above**

The Zimmer Sports coupé is another Fiero special built by the Zimmer Motors Company in Florida. They took a new Fiero V6 and lengthened the car about six inches before cladding it with their own unique body work and fitting a completly new interior. The result is a stylish classic design which makes the converted Fiero stand out in a crowd

**Right**

The Patriot is the car that the Pontiac Fiero could have been. Using a Miller-Woods-built turbocharged Pontiac V6, the Patriot develops a conservative 226 hp for the mid-engine layout. Fiero components are used underneath the 22-piece moulded kit that is done in either composites of glassfibre or carbon fibre. Adrian Corbett, the Patriot's engineer/designer from Lompoc, California, claims acceleration of 0-60 mph in five seconds and handling comparable to a race car

**Above**

*The engine in the Sport-Tech comes from a Suzuki motorcycle. But it's as much an American hot rod as a '32 Ford Roadster. Put it on a track or skid-pad and the numbers look awfully close to GTP race car figures. A 0-60 mph time of sub-five seconds lets it play with the super cars*

**Left**

*The Sport-Tech at speed is a slick sight to see. Its ground-hugging body work and rounded organic lines make it a flash of light as it streaks along in the Michigan sunshine*

**Above left**
The Festiva from Hell. Beck Developments in Upland, California, call this pocket rocket the 'Shogun'. They removed the puny four-cylinder econo-engine and shoehorned in a 220 hp super-duty Ford SHO V6. Now a trip to the 7-Eleven can be done before you even leave the driveway

**Left**
A Yamaha-built, Ford SHO 220 hp doesn't leave any room for rear seat passengers. It does, however, give a new meaning to the idea of fast delivery with a sub-five second 0-60 mph

**Above**
The 'Gilamonster' from DuoPower in Santa Fe Springs California is a concept car which they hope to build as a limited production luxery roadster. Built on a tubular steel frame around a mid-mounted 500 cubic inch Cadillac V8. The Gilamonster's exotic looking fibreglass body gives it a sophisticated air of confidence and style. The design is the the brainchild of Masao Watanabe whose other cars include the Afghan 5.7 coupé/convertible and the Mercedes 190-based Pandora

**Right**

The AREX (American Roadster Experimental) is a purist's two-seater sports roadster built by Industrial Design Research. Power is provided by a 600 hp, 5.7 litre, twin-turboed, small-block Chevrolet built by the Gale Banks company in Azusa, California. The engine is mid-mounted and attached directly to a ZF five-speed trans-axle. The composite body is bolted to a semi-monocoque/tube frame chassis. Suspension design is simple yet effective, using unequal length A-arms at the front riding on coils with a multi-link, push-rod suspension supported on coil/over shocks in the rear

**Above**

The body of the Arex is built in three sections. The centre section, which uses a semi-monocoque steel tub, houses the passengers in a safety cell. The body is built of composite glassfibre material using a narrow body section with cab-forward styling to house the cockpit. Both riders get body-hugging seating which sits deep alongside the wide centre console. The dash features full analog instrumentation including instantaneous dyno read outs from the trick on-board Banks dyno unit

**Above**

*The Jackrabbit kit is designed for people on a budget who want to have fun and scare ZR-1 Corvettes. The kit is built on a custom steel frame that accepts VW Rabbit or Scirocco components. Since everything bolts on, including the drivetrain, suspension, and wiring, virtually no fabrication is required by the final assembler. Only basic hand tools and average mechanical aptitude are required to assemble the kit which comes in 11 pieces with a roll-bar and top optional*

**Right**

*The Jackrabbit Speedster is the 'bugs in the teeth' version of the Herb Adams homebuilt kit. Around 150 hours are required to assemble the car including a paint job. Once completed, the Speedster with its aluminum chassis and 2-litre 16-valve Volkswagen engine has a power-to-weight ratio that can scare a Ferrari. This hot little number has won numerous kit car 'Shoot outs' It offers a home-builder an easy conversion using simple hand-tools to build a neck-snapping, eye-catching convertible that's as much fun as an automobile that costs five times the price*

**Above**

The W2 Vector was first introduced in the early seventies and promised to be America's newest and fastest exotic. Utilising the traditional American philosophy of a big V8 feeding the rear wheels, a top speed of 240 mph is realized only moments after mashing the accelerator to the floor. The creator and driving force behind the Vector, Gerald Wiegert, began in 1971 to try to achieve his dream of building a V8 supercar that offers all the visceral excitement of a ground-bound jet fighter. First shown in Geneva in 1976, the first running prototype arrived in 1978

**Above right**

The Vector W8 was in development a full 15 years before production was begun. The Vector Aeromotive Corporation in Wilmington, California, started delivering W8 Vectors in early 1991 with a price tag just north of US $420,000. For your money the Vector offers an independent suspension and a 625 hp twin-turbocharged 6.0 litre V8. Gerald Wiegert would not be satisfied if the W8 didn't excel at everything, including safety.

The Vector features twin air bags, massive racing-type disc brakes, a full roll cage and an automatic fire suppression system. The quality of suspension and electrical systems are up to military aircraft specifications

**Right**

The Avtech WX-3 not only adopts a new, more powerful engine, but it receives extensive improvements in other areas as well. The body is completely re-styled from either of the first two cars, utilising softer angles and offering smoother lines. While a myriad of vents and openings are present, each has a function and is quite necessary. The body is constructed of Kevlar, carbon and glass fibre in a resin matrix like the W-8 but a carbon fibre skin is used to save weight. The new chassis is extremely rigid and should offer even more crash protection than the W-8, which, incidentally, passed DOT testing with flying colours. The suspension is being revised and lightened and will now carry 18-inch wheels shod with 245/40ZR and 325/30ZR Michelins front and rear respectively

**Left**

The Consulier is an American sports car that offers the best in performance. Built in Florida, the Consulier combines an extremely lightweight body and a powerful Shelby/Chrysler turbo engine to give an acceleration factor that puts most production cars 'in the box'. Consulier took race car styling to the street with the car using lines similar to those of a GTP race car. This gives the coupé an unusual but functional look. With a true monocoque built of Kevlar and carbon fibre, it uses metal frames only for engine and suspension sub-frames. The benefits of the Sports C4 model are double-fold. Weighing only 1750 lb, it delivers an 8:1 power-to-weight ratio which in turn produces blinding acceleration and allows the car to deliver an equally amazing 34 mpg on the highway

**Above**

The Chrysler Shelby 2.2 litre turbo engine in the Sport C4 Consulier delivers 224 hp when fully optioned. The engine and trans-axle are mounted amidship and can push the C4 from 0-60 mph in less than five seconds and romp home with a top speed of 135 mph. Consulier have run the C4 in the IMSA Supercar series where 200 lb of ballast were added in '91 to slow it down so the other cars could remain competitive. The true performance of the Consulier was shown when a Corvette LT1 attempted to set a record lap time, only to be beaten by four seconds when the Consulier lapped the track in one warm up lap! Quite amazing for a four-cylinder car from a small manufacturing company

Replica Cobra kits are one of America's most popular home-built automobiles. This stunning North American Fiberglass kit was built by Bob Kirkland, a retired Ford executive who wanted to bring the 'good old days' of American sports car performance back to the street. Powered by a 351 cubic inch Cleveland V8, it uses four down-draft 48 mm IDA Weber carburetors to deliver a dyno-tuned 425 hp at 5500 rpm, while a T5 five-speed manual gearbox gets the horses moving. Finished in Guardsman Blue with white stripes, it matches the original '64 Shelby Cobra factory colour scheme